On Unfirm Terrain

On Unfirm Terrain

Poems by

Christina E. Petrides

© 2022 Christina E. Petrides. All rights reserved.
This material may not be reproduced in any form, published,
reprinted, recorded, performed, broadcast,
rewritten or redistributed without
the explicit permission of Christina E. Petrides.
All such actions are strictly prohibited by law.

Cover design by Shay Culligan
Cover art by Nika Tchaikovskaya

ISBN: 978-1-63980-220-3

Kelsay Books
502 South 1040 East, A-119
American Fork, Utah 84003
Kelsaybooks.com

To E.E.W.T.,
who doesn't understand why I like to travel,
or much of what I write,
but loves me anyway.

Acknowledgments

Grateful acknowledgement is made to the editors of these journals, where the following poems appeared, some in earlier versions:

2018
Anak Sastra: "Indonesian Swamp," "PC Room"
Better Than Starbucks! Poetry Magazine: "Insomnia"

2019
Adelaide Literary Magazine: "Old Salt," "Barista," "Precaution"
all the sins: "Witch Trial"
The Charles Carter: "Waiting"
Eratio: "Unlicensed," "Rush Hour," "Naptime Ritual"
Former People: "Lights in Osaka," "Seoul Metro II"
Grey Sparrow Journal: "Storm Brewing"
Halcyon Days: "Clouds"

2020
Boned: "After the Storm"
Brief Wilderness: "Crossed Culture"
The Courtship of Winds: "Pea Picking"
Dream Noir: "Pressure," "Pep Talk"
Eastern Structures: "Aftermath"
From Sac: "Unreasonable"
Gingerbread House Literary Magazine: "Captive Fruit"
Haikuniverse: "Fruitless Effort"
Harbinger Asylum: "My Funeral," "Pastures"
Kathmandu Tribune: "Seoul Metro I," "Moon," "At the DMZ"
Life and Legends: "Decomposition," "The Duel"
Modern Literature: "Drugstore Blues," "Seogwipo Harbor," "Matchmaker," "The Introvert's Dilemma"
The Nonconformist Magazine: "Fall"

2021
CP (Crêpe & Penn) Quarterly: "3 AM"
The Decadent Review: "March in Jeju"
The Ganga Review: "Making Do"
The Headlight Review: "Korean Winter"
Hive Avenue Literary Journal: "Common Oddity"
In Parentheses: "Fate," "Jeju Weather," "Good Fight," "Concrete Memory," "Weekend Morning," "Corporate Lagomorph"
Kathmandu Tribune: "Sleeping Alone," "Summer," "Endurance," "The Test," "Exoskeleton"
Lullwater Review: "Commencement"
Night Picnic: "Recalcitrant," "A Golf Legend," "Growing Plans," "Six-Legged Conspiracy," "An Average Morning"
Nōd Magazine: "Street Market"
North Dakota Quarterly: "Online Auction," "Changing Weather"
Nude Bruce Review: "After"
October Hill Magazine: "Political Animal"
Oddball Magazine: "Memes Old & New"
The Opiate: "First Kiss," "Narcissi"
The Pangolin Review: "Fleeting Wisdom"
Round Table Literary Journal: "Japanese Mall," "Jeju Shore II," "Bangtan Corps"
Sheepshead Review: "Japan in Transit," "The Adventuress"
The South Shore Review: "Jeju Field," "Jeju Disposal"
Wingless Dreamer (anthology): "Life Story"

2022
The Garfield Lake Review: "Unfaded," "Reflection"
Modern Poets Magazine: "Fusion," "Fishbowl," "Unsettled," "Osaka Impressions"

Contents

Indonesian Swamp	15
PC Room	15
Picnic	15
Smack	16
Japan in Transit	16
Transformation	16
Japanese Mall	17
Lights in Osaka	17
Osaka Impressions	18
At the DMZ	18
Russian Train	19
Seoul Metro I	20
Seoul Metro II	20
Korean Winter	21
De/Construction	21
Ocean View	22
Jeju Shore	22
Jeju Field	23
Break	23
Jeju Disposal	24
Pastures	24
Seogwipo Harbor	25
March in Jeju	25
Fishbowl	26
Concrete Memory	26
Jeju Weather	27
Storm Brewing	27
Tradecraft	27
Fall	28
Aftermath	28
Outburst	28
After the Storm	29
Changing Weather	29

Clouds	30
Good Fight	30
Growing Plans	31
Exoskeleton	31
Six-Legged Conspiracy	32
Plastic Bag	32
Old Salt	32
Our Business	33
Witch Trial	34
Pressure	35
Unfaded	35
Reflection	36
Modern Hydra	36
Self-Respect	36
The Adventuress	37
Fate	37
Weekend Morning	38
An Average Morning	38
Simulacrum	39
Decomposition	39
S/he Says	39
Leadership	40
Online Auction	40
Narcissi	41
Unlicensed	42
Commencement	42
Endurance	42
Pep Talk	43
Fleeting Wisdom	43
Corporate Lagomorph	44
Unsettled	44
Waiting	45

Brows	46
First Kiss	46
Crossed Culture	47
Sleeping Alone	47
Unreasonable	48
After	48
Words	49
Common Oddity	49
Matchmaker	50
The Introvert's Dilemma	50
Fruitless Effort	51
Pea Picking	51
Captive Fruit	51
Drugstore Blues	52
Soul Food	52
Rush Hour	53
Dream Tree	53
Candy	53
Summer	54
A Golf Legend	54
Life Story	55
My Funeral	56
Precaution	56
Street Market	57
Clarification	57
The Test	58
Requiem	58
Recalcitrant	59
Cat Sick	59
Moon	60
Naptime Ritual	60
Fusion	60

The Duel	61
Political Animal	61
Memes Old & New	62
Insomnia	62
Dad Jokes	63
Personal Library	63
Barista	63
Bangtan Corps	64
Sweet	64
Southern Barbeque	64
Possession	65
Making Do	66

Indonesian Swamp

A fat dappled snake twists on a muddy riverbank.
Slime-stained slender paddles push
into blackness beneath
ancient moss-specked trees.
A rotten log or hungry crocodile bumps
the thin bottom of the canoe.
The tourist sits frozen, drifting silently
until the monster sinks invisible behind her.
Moist air seethes with mosquitoes.
Startled turtles dive into green water,
and birds call in fear—
a flock bursts skyward in a cloud of frantic flapping wings.

PC Room

Outside air steams
with the memories of centuries
of rice farms overbuilt with glass and steel
high-rises and bright heat of traffic.
In a dark room no creature stirs but
bandwidth vampires—
glowing, awkward,
hunched and typing furiously.
My skirt curls in a breeze
from the air conditioner
like a cat winding around my ankles.

Picnic

Midday shadows
of spring trees
tattoo the grass.

Smack

Caress my bare neck—
I'll slap hard enough to kill.
Get lost, mosquito!

Japan in Transit

Surgeons' masks and gloveless hands
on bicycles carve fast striding winter crowds
that collide at clanking intersections
whose lights bleed out green to red.
Walkers and riders and drivers stop just short
of fringe-jointed gates and bells that block
cold pavements from speeding trains.
Sliding over oily rails on thick velvet benches,
passengers sit against viewing windows
or stand plastic-cuffed and ready to break
onto chilly platforms and through thronged tunnels
to reach the narrow confines of mat-floored apartments
and sorely-earned white cotton *shikibuton*.*

*shikibuton: a traditional Japanese sleeping mattress

Transformation

Sporting the nonstick wrinkle-free smolder
and patented lip curl of the sexiest poster idol,
he steps out fresh—neck prickling, sideburns razor sharp,
bangs blown and gelled into an artfully casual tousle—
an uncouth pigeon grown briefly dignified
until traffic, dust, and heat wilt him again
into an average middle-aged salaryman.

Japanese Mall

Petite pale girls on black stacked shoes
wade through torrents of humanity.
They eddy in department stores,
rush through corridors between underground trains,
and pool around bright restaurants advertising
sake, sushi, Kobe beef, and drowned udon.
Bare-tailed battered plastic shrimp float
anchored in plain ceramic bowls
beyond glass rinsed spotless several times a day,
and tall young men in white aprons proffer elegant menus
to lure these uncertain shoals to dine.

Lights in Osaka

The awkward tympani played by
an ancient metal clown in candy prison stripes
launched today's spinning, twinkling, burning,
universal molten motion.
Opposite an oval tracked Ferris wheel
crowds pour under waving crab legs
local lore credits to a man on a bicycle
who couldn't pass the busy streets
that parallel the canal where
local baseball fans drowned Colonel Sanders
following a since-unrepeated victory.
Innumerable screens glow
on selfie sticks, line pachinko parlors,
and promise sales, deals,
discounts, specials, and brand names
in complex confusions of symbols and letters
to dazzled foreign visitors while
new lovers stroll oblivious
to all but their glued hands.

Osaka Impressions

It had been forty years
since I had seen a cigarette vending machine.

It sat on the street with the other automats,
outside a shop with narrow stairs,
in a neighborhood of close-cropped pines,
sliding partitions between tatami floors,
claustrophobic fiberglass baths,
and heated-seat high-tech toilets.

A short walk further on,
workers in smart dark uniforms waved off
precisely timed trains packed with salarymen and shoppers
from covered arcades of overbright fake food,
costly dishware, clothes, cosmetics,
all still mesmerized by neon and flashing lights.

At the DMZ

Wheeling songbirds soar free
above three score years' lost mines.
Endangered beasts limp through wilds
barred from bussed-in tourists
that gawk at distant concrete ruins,
deserted and grainy in magnified smog.
Smartphone-bereft camouflaged youths
trudge paths of rusted razor wire,
and shift well-oiled guns to wave
at skinny soldiers on the other side,
who sit grim and silent in stilted huts,
all wary of a long-postponed explosion.

Russian Train

A golden horde of dandelions
rides across a fallow field,
the train—rocking with electric steam—
slides into summer woods.

Through the glass,
birch trees telegraph dots and dashes,
reeling out silver-screen flashes
through pale green leaves.

Kerchiefs bob amid deep ferns.
Wild mushrooms overflow wicker baskets.

Passengers sway gently
to the steel rails' slow percussion.

A man holds a bouquet of roses.

Wafting dust transforms each flower.
An ancient church shines in the waning light.

Its domes have cracked like tsar's eggs,
and incense clouds the air.

Past nightfall, tired arrivals
pull luggage towards gaping exits,
while cheerful crowds board sleeping cars
from bright concrete platforms.

Early tomorrow,
local lines will fill with distracted adults,
eager children, and wriggling pets
outbound for dacha weekends.

Seoul Metro I

Yawning brakes
slide to soft stops.
Black puffy coats
crush together.
Rubber-rimmed doors
bang-clamp shut.
Silent triangles swing,
tuned to the rhythm
of distant thunder
and the flashes
of fluorescence
in the tunnels.
Trains shriek
and whirr warmly,
crashing through darkness,
wriggling spasms
within the pregnant city.

Seoul Metro II

Untouched triangles swing from the bright steel rod bolted to the
ceiling.
Precise female voices intone successive languages.
Riders subside further into warm molded plastic seats
as more black coats crowd the car.
Masked and gloved in winter anonymity,
some stare out blind windows, mumbling one-sided dialogues,
their quiet words sucked away by short ear straws.
Other immobile travelers, intent on their phones,
stand deaf to the shocks of the train,
reading silently of scandals or playing fast-paced games
with intimate strangers.

Korean Winter

The full moon glows in a sky
mostly clear of clouds.
The wind whistles like a hot teakettle
and kicks up curlicues of snow
tens of meters into the air
from the half-inch on the ground.
The frozen crystals bite my ankles,
bombard the lenses of my glasses,
and reach into my hood to tap my stiff ears.
Under the streetlights, embers of Pluto's fire
dance backwards as I reach home.
The hall lights switch on automatically
as I pull off my glove. The lock snaps back.
I numbly shed my shoes at the threshold,
and step in stocking-feet onto the *ondol,**
which immediately melts my icy toes.
I drop my coat, bag, and then to my knees,
and am soon stretched like a sunbathing cat
on the quilted rug, determined to absorb
every delicious particle of warmth.

*ondol: the traditional Korean floor-heating system

De/Construction

Mated to keyboards,
stubborn parasites
breed electric worlds
while outdoors
cement mixers tear
petals from exhausted trees,
unbuilding springtime.

Ocean View

Small polystyrene globes
sift off eroded cliffs
to float on lost soles
and bloated plastic bags.
Metallic fish are trapped
among cigarette and candy wrappers.
Octopi caress the ragged edges
of old cans and tangled nets.
Children run on beaches
around shattered glass
and sandy soda straws.
When did our human prospects
become so unnaturally troublesome?

Jeju Shore

A lanky burnt-orange tomcat
scales the cratered cliff,
and disappears into a thicket.

Bright-jacketed twins
shout among boulders
of found shells and small creatures.

Shadowed anglers wait
for abruptly swaying lines
to signal a catch.

Buoyed by waves, seagulls
watch for threats and food,
hunted and hunting.

Jeju Field

From unmown grasses
drying in early autumn
trill three-note insects.
Short palms shed frayed burlap.

Tiny blue butterflies
dodge gangly dandelions,
trefoil clovers, wild lettuces,
and the claws of small cattails.

Squeaks pinwheel
in the breeze
that sweeps the evergreens
and vines tying hidden snares.

Convict crickets file their cages,
while feathery and hollow
silver-plumed grasses resist
pulling tassels from their sleeves.

A blue farm truck
coughs in the lane frilled
with discarded plastic lids and bags
from the nearby eco-resort.

Break

The laborer stares into the middle distance.
He drops a swollen hand to his bent knees,
thumb-flicks a bit of ash,
and exhales a silver stream.
Begrudgingly, he grasps a stained shovel,
and levers up to work,
leaving the tobacco smoldering in the sandy dirt.

Jeju Disposal

Orange public compost boxes chatter
in the sunshine by trash and recycling bins
parked on residential streets.
Tempted with a token card, their square lids gape
for pails of peelings, wilted fruit, and table scraps.
In the lighted alcoves after dark, old men sit on camp stools.
They watch soapy dramas and eye passersby,
ready to bark at those who ignore enormous, faded banners
that declare specific days for paper, days for glass,
for plastic bottles, wrappers, Styrofoam, and metal.
At midnight these crusty guards ride off on creaking bicycles.
Then stray cats and rubbish scofflaws sneak out
with empty bellies and full bags,
and torn illicit piles overspill the bins at dawn.

Pastures

Barks shudder the drum-stretched hollows
of a starved brown dog in the sun.
The collision camera in a shiny shade-parked truck
also blinks a warning to potential vandals.
The voices of imported laborers
mutter from fresh-tilled fields nearby.
They sweat, rolling out bolts of thick plastic,
securing it with pockmarked rocks,
while well-groomed local hikers enjoy pleasant
weekend weather on the passing trail.

Seogwipo Harbor

The silver sky razors the gunmetal sea.

A small trawler churns around the barrier island,
cutting a wake that subsides shiny smooth
between a parked Coast Guard vessel alongside the outer pier
and concrete block warehouses at the town's threshold
that emit a constant refrigeration hum.

The single missile pylon of the pedestrian bridge pierces
the sail that billows from the harbor side,
welcoming fierce winds that forever rush shoreward.

Snowy seabirds skim the ripple-mirrored water
between moored fishing boats with faded blue mildewed hulls
and yellow bumpers dangling from bow and stern.

Cars mumble up the curved road from the docks,
and small songbirds chatter in short-needled evergreens.

Through the plateau park, relaxed adults trail happy dogs
and masked children in the cool and peaceful afternoon.

March in Jeju

Awkward gusts shove pedestrians,
elbow them and send their parcels flying,
whine around uncovered ears,
scatter leaves and roll rubbish,
rattle metal traffic signs,
make the streetlights bounce,
and tear at blue construction scrims.
Chatty, blustery, self-confident, brash:
reckless teenaged winds in spring.

Fishbowl

A red silk goldfish swims at the window
overlooking our central roundabout
filled with wandering white rental cars
and gurgling island buses that sink
to rest at several transfer stops.
Schools of pedestrians flash
green bottles and shiny bags
as they glide along the sidewalks.
Delivery motorbikes dart through
the traffic and the crowds.
Old men slowly pick up litter from
among the rocks and beneath the trees
undulating with the traffic current.

Concrete Memory

The curb outside my workplace
reflects my tired shadow.
I lean over the plastic caution tape
to touch the new pavement, leaving dents
too shallow to catch rain or tears.
One summer twilight two score years ago
Daddy carried me in my flannel pajamas
down to the pale backyard slab
to press my small heels and toes
beside my uncle's wide handprint.
Granddaddy scrawled name and date
with a sticky green pine twig.
That faint impression remains after
our own irrefutable change.

Jeju Weather

I dreamed of walking alone at night
before the sidewalks
froze and the cold
seeped into the bones
of the buildings
and left us shivering
beside space heaters
under heavy blankets.

Then I awoke to pelting summer rain.

Storm Brewing

A squall of seabirds rises
from the rock broken surf.
White foam and feathers
brilliant in the sun
cascade again
onto the restless water.

A fleet of dull grey ships
sits serene on the horizon.
Each vessel smoothly turns
empty eyes shoreward
and awaits a clear signal
to open fire.

Tradecraft

The best way to out
an American spy? Sneeze.
S/he can't but "Bless you!"

Fall

Fortune turns
her spiked wheel
twisting bones
tongue in groove

soft caramel
charred red sand
glass darkly
reflects pain

needle leaves
change colors
sharp winds trace
branch edges

Aftermath

Glittering snow steams
amidst a wrecked transport truck
on sun-bleached asphalt.
Skinned bodies lie torn from stakes.
Their wet bark hangs in rough shreds.

Outburst

Heavy storm clouds poured
their pent-up frustrations
on unwary fields. Afterwards,
the near-ripe grain hung
in limp embarrassment,
its green shoulders turned
against the coaxing sun.

After the Storm

Skeletons of skinned umbrellas
snatched and eaten midflight
litter the sidewalk
with leaves and branches.
Rags snarl the corners
of stepping stones.
A torrent of white water
tumbles down the spillway.
Scores of sea roaches
frisk about the sunny beach.
Dark clouds throw themselves
at the northward mountain.

Changing Weather

This morning my window was scattered with raindrops,
silver on the glass before a soft grey sky.
There were puddles on the flat rooftops
under sagging lines of dripping laundry.
I bagged my notebooks, then punched up
my umbrella against continuous drizzle.
Only an hour after I started work,
the clouds drifted off over the ocean
and the white sun beamed down.
The small children in my class
missed a rainbow in the afternoon.

Clouds

Nimble nimbus
dripping water

Subtle stratus
trending higher

Middling altos
acclimate

Wispy cirrus
dissipate

Fat cumulus
forge dark magic
or drift luminous
serene and classic

Good Fight

Resist? Resist. Resist!
Push back with all your might
against the undoing and the doing
which breed fear and death.
Seize pain's passing lessons.
Demand its deep knowledge—
for each dislocation wring from it
a generous promise.
Downcast days can blind us
or train our stubbornness
to see flickers of light
from ancient explosions
reverberate into the future.

Growing Plans

Man, hey, that's so cool
your dad wants you to come home
to open a pot dispensary!

A father-son joint venture
may flourish,
or the profits go up in smoke
as unbanked grass attracts attention.
You want to blunt some common ills,
but other creatures could crawl out
to eat the bowls of nectar you prepare.

I wish I had a crystal or a magic torch
to diffuse the future's haze to tell
whether the strain may be an ounce too much
or if you'll emerge solvent in a season,
oil dripping down your heirloom hippy beards.

In any case, bud,
wish you the best!

Exoskeleton

Spider legs wave
over bones slowly rising
out of huge, webbed coffin-holes.
Thin jointed pipes inject
grey syrup into forms,
bricking up the sky with hives,
antennae buried deep.
Glued in place to desiccate,
they glitter empty-eyed—
nests of frantic drones
rearranging toxic sand.

Six-Legged Conspiracy

a bottle-green fly squatted
outside her window
on the air conditioning unit
to rub its forefeet together

chuckling
it buzzed off
and the enamel ladybug charm
on her bracelet grinned sinisterly

after five days
the fire ants that had invaded
the chocolate in her pantry
began to eat her as well

Plastic Bag

Rebellious, raven-winged
above the busy street,
refusing earth's static call,
the thin suffocating skin
beats on exhausted gusts—
a headless manmade portent
of oncoming death and war.

Old Salt

Flushed from alcohol, wind and weather,
and grooved from age,
The woman clutches her fishing rod and glares at the sea.
It twinkles back at her
and crashes unconcerned into the rocks below.

Our Business

We didn't mean to kill you.

We just had some questions—
we were going to suggest (politely)
that you change your tone,
persuade you—gently—to recant
all the harsh things you've said.

Our outrage suddenly boiled over.

How could you so
impudently challenge us?
Why did you oppose our accepted
status quo antediluvian?

And such a widespread fuss
over an alleged restraint,
so much complaint
at your supposed death!

Why bother only now,
when these events
have been safely-ignored
domestic matters for so long?

Witch Trial

What craft is this?
His contempt snakes like angry spittle along her forehead.
Her interrogator sneers
at the lace at her neck—
sorcery to seduce unwitting men,
every thread of her designed to deceive,
to pull the innocent from the ladder
of improvement,
pluck them from the arduous climb to the small casement
that may welcome them like a lover
or slam sharply at their last mortal breath.

He knows her heart wanders like her wet eyes,
that the turn of her wrist, the bones of her little finger entice—
although everything else is thickly swaddled,
her steps muffled and awkward,
her speech timid and reactive.
Somehow without paint she is a jezebel
born into subtle politics,
a temptress so wily that
her own abilities are beyond her understanding.
Her short, unpolished nails are talons
to sink into the hearts of the unwary.

She is small, plain, obscure, poor—
she can surely possess neither heart nor soul—
and so she is despised
even as she is feared.

Pressure

To be silenced
is to be discouraged.
Stifled dreams seep away
to poison air, earth,
and people.
Unrealized ambitions,
thwarted hopes,
and muted prayers seethe
until they burst
into enraged action—
blind, fierce, and embittered.

Unfaded

I lightly shake hands
and pretend
to recall nothing
of the prowling senior
in the lab that night,
a moment that
rots my bruised soul
and claws the edges
of my thoughts. Still,
I won't sacrifice my pride
to public scrutiny
which cannot understand
what marks us
is never really passed.

Reflection

What see you in the mirror, heart?
A damsel in distress, an aged crone,
or perhaps a wily fox of fable?
Some knightly mouse from legend,
rescuing lions? Or a beast herself
ensnared by princely pride,
plunged afoul the crotchety fairy
who, consulting an eccentric pool,
sews kingdoms in thickets
of mystery and fearsome vegetation?
Or in the glass do you shine silver,
a creator of charming magic,
fiercely guarding innocence
from encroachments of gloom?

Modern Hydra

The power supply's alternate endings
for charging multiple brands' devices
prickled her damp skin as she clutched
her smartphone to her bosom and prayed
to the SNS gods for the perfect emoji.

Self-Respect

We stubbornly prevail,
eschewing exes' posts
that proffer glimpses
of repulsively happy lives.

The Adventuress

She refused to be put upon.
She simply did everything
no one thought to mention was impossible.
It wasn't a matter of overcoming,
but of her always moving towards the sun.
The world was her pearl, her unexplored ocean floor,
and she dove into action as if born flying.
Her spiritual household numbered in the thousands,
she maintained a dozen friends, and kept no lovers.
Many would have followed her if they could;
her path was too swift and terrible for ordinary men.
For her struggling sisters she cut a bright trail of what could be
when fearless passion guides an unfettered life.

Fate

Has life boiled down
to golden goose eggs
in one basket
obliterated
by slow-rolling
rush hour traffic;
a glistening slime
tired workers track
across sidewalks
suffering acid rain?
Or do you see in weeds
crawling up from
cracked pavement
an omen of your struggle,
a promised renaissance
despite all attempts
to blot you out?

Weekend Morning

I do not want to get out of bed.

Sure, there are loads of things to do,
from laundry to grocery shopping—
tasks put off from workdays.

But that would mean getting up;
getting dressed;
going outside into the biting cold.

And I am so comfortable lying here in my pajamas.

A sabbath sun filters gently through the frosted window
and reassures me that I can nap with impunity.

An Average Morning

Strumming my ribs and patting my belly like a drum
I stare at nothing through the window
before shuffling off to wash my face
with the hand soap beside the sink
and poke around in my closet to choose
one well-worn black outfit among others.
I leave the house, only to be startled at a reflection
in a shopfront glass on the short walk to work—
Who is that frumpy female carrying my purse,
and how did she forget to brush her hair?!

Simulacrum

Though photographed from all angles,
squeezed, filtered, primped and posed
to look her best online (if not in person),
she knew little of herself. The curated
albums hid an empty core—the once-fresh
fruit petrified, shocked into a silent shell
by the never-ending electronic buzz
that branded her influential.

Decomposition

She recalls the rainbow on a puddle,
engine oil spreading thin and iridescent,
winking at the wider world that afternoon
before ignorant tires drove through,
splashing droplets that swiftly dried on the pavement.
Dust motes waver in the heat from the lamp bulb,
glimmering threads pass through existence in a breath.
She chews her pen end and inhales numbered perfume
from the sticky resin on her face and neck,
knowing her passing attempts at freezing time
in person or in print would one day evaporate.

S/he Says

He thinks they're speaking
the same language. She contends
word meanings differ.

Leadership

How can you be to work inclined
in droning sessions when you find
an inverse cleft, a mutant pock
high on your cheek? The swell's a shock.

Absorbed, you tap your bulging skin,
to estimate the pus within.
Your colleagues talk *ad nauseum*
concerning an emporium.

You pretend to focus blankly—
and pinch the turgid yellow top
of your adolescent acne.
There's an unprepossessing "pop."

Sideburn patting with a tissue
is your newest staff-wide issue:
"Boss, are you okay? You're bleeding . . ."
"Fine. Let's end our weekly meeting."

Online Auction

Bid now or forever regret
the offer you did not make;
the few pennies
you failed to risk to win
that bauble of cherished memory
you heedlessly threw away
or an item you once could not afford
(now used and grossly out of date).
Each has become a gritty, chipped trophy
of your mature triumph.

Narcissi

He stumbled slowly through the crowd
that floated high on pills and pot,
when all at once girls gasped aloud,
"Oh god, what the—that man's been shot!"
Beside the stage, amidst the screams,
falt'ring and bleeding through his jeans.

Countless as post-use plastic waste
that clogs the oceans day and night
their phones came out to film and haste
the news to contacts off the site;
ten million saw it at a glance,
while scrolling feeds in mindless trance.

Reports slew patrons straight away;
within that awful battery,
a witness, physically okay,
saw their assailant on one knee:
"He blazed away without a sound,
a vacant stare behind each round."

At home upon a sofa stretched
binge-watching shows in solitude
we hear the chimes from SNS
that interrupt th' obsessive mood;
and then our heart with terror thrills,
and trembles at the camera stills.

Unlicensed

angry shadows
drive down
smoke-crowded promenades
to maim strangers
shatter common peace
cut to weeping ribbons of police tape
and makeshift blankets
to fan fears of greater dangers
blowing up

Commencement

A dirty mattress leans into the weeds
where a buxom cut-out blonde hoists a frothy mug,
and mismatched kitchenware lies by the peeling carport door.
What the old house expelled
with its most recent youthful occupants
awaits belated county trucks or trespassing scavengers.

Endurance

You wish you had
its stubborn streak—
the engagingly perverse
ability to thrive
despite regular trauma.
In crevices, on grout, in drains,
in damp, in heat, in stinking toilets,
showers, baths, and sinks, it endures.
Resolute against all
sophistication,
it always blooms again,
triumphant mold.

Pep Talk

Knock it back to good old times square one.
Show them what you're made of—
not jelly donuts & egg-dipped toast,
but vinegar and spit.
Lift up the bristled chin
that greets your morning makeup mirror,
and don't give into a deceitful broken heart.
Take peace into your troubled mind
(spare a thought for fools and little children in harm's way),
and for the rest—easy does it.
Put your shoulder to the grindstone,
but don't hurt yourself.
That's what I would do, if I were you.

Fleeting Wisdom

That cold porcelain seat is called "the throne"
since so many insights into deep philosophy
and bursts of creative stimulation come when
doing business of a fundamental sort. Perched
like a potentate, you gaze at the checkered tiles,
your mind divinely clear and forming fine ideas
from which you may be torn and flushed away
the moment you reach for the multi-ply roll.

Corporate Lagomorph

There is nothing quite like a huge ice cold
carrot after a long stint listening
to warm, well-intentioned colleagues
rabbit on in meetings when you'd rather
be napping underneath a leafy tree.
Grey wolves snuffle around the box
where you nibble, innocently concealed.
Those highly caffeinated suits
will tear you to shreds if you emerge
from your burrow before sundown.

Unsettled

We are imperfect friends, you and I—
each occasionally disrupting the other's plans,
sources of periodic irritation and frequent bewilderment.
I did not imagine that our long-anticipated parting would discomfit
me so.
I am scared.
I had thought about your leaving in abstract terms,
but now we know the day.
You are busy tidying, tying up loose ends,
meeting people for what could be the last time,
expressing grave thanks.
Insomnia lurks near my bed.
It waits for me to conclude my evening ritual
and compose myself for sleep.
Then, it settles in beside me,
all sharp elbows and stage whispers,
filling the space and hours with worry
about how my life will look alone.

Waiting

To be briefly assessed
by an ordinary American physician
requires a stint in purgatory.
Compared, the oft-bemoaned Post Office line
resembles a bullet train to paradise.
In patient seating areas,
industrial fluorescent rods glow overhead,
sickening dingy upholstery
and covers of expired magazines,
their pages curled by countless unwashed hands.
Stilted soap opera dialogs and rapacious lawyer ads
drip from the eternal television.
Clerks who dimly comprehend
only the operation of the telephone
wear surgical scrubs.
Those personnel not chained to desks
prod unwilling visitors' mental sores
by reshuffling them among
increasingly featureless rooms
to the frustrating mantra
"Please wait here,
the doctor will see you shortly."
So grim lifetimes pass slowly by.

Brows

Poisonous caterpillars,
shed roofs, downy streaks,
velvet patches, twin arches.
Penciled, painted,
teased, tweezed.
Flirtatious, condemnatory,
quizzical, shocked.
Chemically removed,
biologically immobilized.
Bushy, barely visible,
untamed, unified.
We say and do so much with those
odd lines of fur above our eyes.

First Kiss

Her first kiss was nothing like the movies'.
There were no swelling symphonies,
soft glowing lights or slow-motion spins.
He was neither royal nor redeemed.
Their lips stumbled in rigid inexperience,
and unlike magnets or puzzle pieces,
they did not fit perfectly together.
His heart raced. Hers did not,
yet she detailed the unprecedented moment
in a raw message to a longsuffering friend.

Crossed Culture

You told me to stop bowing—
yet each polite bend brought me closer to the untouchable:
you, another's lover.
I'd like to believe we share glances of mute passion,
or have I misread commonplaces
as breathing coded ardor?
Do you really want to draw me to your heart
as earnestly as I yearn to be pulled?
and if so, must we always remain stiffly at arms' length?

Sleeping Alone

So many songs lament a single sleeper in a double bed
and fail to celebrate the bliss of rest
in such uncluttered space.
There, abundant pillows nestle in your arms
and cup your weary head.
You can snuggle unreservedly
into the comforter's embrace.
It and other linen need not be shared,
but piled high or flung aside at will.
Each night you luxuriate in a great bear-sized nest,
and mornings you may linger, happily tucked in.

Unreasonable

I believed I was immune to charm,
that my intellect
would insulate me
from the soft warm touch,
the gentle word,
and the steady gaze that melts
and leaves me breathless
and insatiable,
a clawing nest of unanticipated
needs and unsettled thoughts
that tumble
over one another
in a tangle of lips and limbs,
mocking the neatness
of my well-ordered life
before I met you.

After

He had been a lucky guy.

In early morning, he walked down
to where full tide licked the rocks.
He stared at boats and birds,
then ate sashimi on a sandy street paved with cigarette butts.

At orange and purple sunset,
he climbed to a stale rented room
to swallow boxed wine out of a paper coffee cup,
sitting sleepless in the chair beside their empty bed.

Words

On a workday metro corner
change and wadded paper
fall from sympathetic suits
to the unkempt mute
with a handwritten appeal.
At weekend slams
that full heart speaks
the life invisibly inked
on his discolored sign.

Common Oddity

People in love act like it is the most normal thing in the world
when it's completely and utterly bizarre.
How do dissimilar individuals come to share a mutual attraction—
moreover, to express those feelings so the other understands?
That seems a marvel beyond marvels for me.
To have one's affections requited?
In what universe does this happen?
To be drawn to someone who is not repulsed by you,
but who even shares a similar enthusiasm, is remarkable.
Such an astounding circumstance deserves to be celebrated
for the miracle it is.

Matchmaker

Across the table out front
they are engrossed in each other,
the guy with earlobe plugs
and the tattoo-splattered girl.

For more than an hour
the two have been immersed
in fervent conversation,
oblivious to their surroundings.

Behind the bar their cupid
silently eats garbanzos
and breaded fish patties
cut out in dinosaur shapes.

His pride at having made
this fresh connection hasn't
offset the gnawing hunger
from his own recent breakup.

The Introvert's Dilemma

Whose monochrome nose
is swollen in the fisheye
of my electric doorbell camera?
A bearer of anticipated packages
or a dreadfully determined apostle
of some pamphlet gospel?
Perhaps if I pretend I am not at home
she or he will go away.
But it may be a neighbor needing help—
a grave emergency. Still,
I will wait until blood or smoke
seeps across the threshold.

Fruitless Effort

The bathroom wall fan
spins dust between mildewed tile
and bright open sky.

Pea Picking

The breeze turns a wobbly wheel of crickets
And blades on the tin windmill clatter

He drops his fork onto his close-scraped plate
And gulps the last sweet mouthful of iced tea

The blue truck idles outside the screen door
While a lazy late summer sun burns overhead

He reapplies his wide brimmed hat
Rolls down his stained cotton sleeves

Whitewall tires bump through grey dust
Where purple hulls hang from limber vines

Captive Fruit

One plump orange, enclosed in thick amphibian skin,
requires three days' dark patience
to release its flavorful peak.
Peppery spots fleck another,
like it rolled across an island's black sand beach,
or was blasted by a sneeze from a small sniffling dragon—
the same clawed beast, no doubt, that bruised yesterday's banana
and left it split to the flesh, fashionably naked
on the red polyester rug before the kitchen sink.

Drugstore Blues

My grandma noisily swigged dregs
of chocolate shake through a limp straw.
Flavored milk filmed her empty glass.
"I'm playing the drugstore blues,"
she declared in satisfaction,
recalling shiny fountains
and white-coated soda jerks
who politely pulled thick syrups
a monochrome midcentury away
from the machined sweets
and imported household goods
that line today's fluorescent aisles.

Soul Food

Each culture has a food that fuels
warm belonging even when eaten alone.
We American Southerners love vivid greens, black-eyed peas,
chicken fried until its floured skin is crispy brown,[*]
and golden cornbread dripping butter and honey.
Half a world away, South Koreans spoon in bubbling broth
thickened by cut-up kimchi, threaded with fresh egg,
and slurp wavy strands of steaming spiced ramen.
On either side is welcome home.

[*]South Koreans have lately come to adore fried chicken, too, but paired with frothy beer. This combination is called *chi-maek*.

Rush Hour

Horns—deep, light, and piercing—
burst through the blur of evening
against the cram school windows
where uniformed students sit
muttering over vocabulary books,
trying to absorb strange foreign words.
Frustrated adults drive homeward,
their tired and wrinkled minds
on those uncompleted mundane duties
left behind or waiting uneasily at home.

Dream Tree

In Korean, a poem (시) is like a seed (씨).
The kernel—an idea's essence
bound up in an unassuming package—
when planted and watered,
begins to send out roots, then shoots
from which green leaves unfurl.
It may produce a delicate flower,
or grow tall and tough, into a great tree (나무),
which shades perspiring dreamers and fruits
untold other seeds which go on multiplying
lyrics of their own.

Candy

Gooey sweet creature
stuck between my molars:
my favorite vice.

Summer

I swing out again over the river,
arcing high and weightless
above the water, rocks, and reeds
that spin beneath my crossed feet.
My braid flies behind me
and my hands hold tight to the rope
creaking across the solid branch.
Too soon, I drop back
towards the knotted bank
and the shoe-scuffed slope
where my sister waits her turn.

A Golf Legend

Rumor has it the rich cabal which controls
the legendary local links
annually sacrifices a nubile caddy
when the moon most resembles
a pale pebbled ball.
The soul of that white-clad clubs-bearer
ensures the weather continues perfect
and the grounds unnaturally exquisite
for the yearly Tournament.
In exchange, his family's name is written
on the long-closed golden list
of those life-elect allowed to purchase tickets—
which divine reward ensures an indefinite
supply of filial votaries.

Life Story

I am a breath.
I will disappear as if I had never been.
Sentimental stone inscribed with my name will crumble in time
and the few who knew me also die.

The brevity of life is tragic.
Its struggles and pains preoccupy me:
is there worth to being and action?

If we are only the latest in improbable successions
of infinite coincidences,
relationships are meaningless,
and existence is futile;
whether we visit evil or good
on our generation and the next
is incidental.

But if we were created, even dark moments—
those others don't appreciate or recall—
have meaning.
And the joys we achieve and share
with our small circles of family and acquaintances
are just mild glimmers of great promised bliss.

That we hate and we love,
that we admire and revile,
that we tell flawed anecdotes,
imperfectly communicated,
and that we recognize depression and elation,
testify to existence apart
from space and time we occupy.

I am a syllable in a great narrative.
What each human is—
with or without a single breath—
contributes to that tale.

My Funeral

No mourning hordes will rush my coffin,
no tearful masses lie buried
under a mad crush of wailing bodies
reaching blindly towards mine,
but a few grizzled bearers pace
unmetered towards a baize blanket
that marks the pit awaiting my oblong box.
The backhoe which built a mound of Georgia clay
will sit a little way off, behind a largish tree, ignored
by obligatory family members and old friends
who sit on folding chairs beneath a tent
and listen to well-worn verses on new life
recited fervently by a dark-suited young man
whose name I cannot remember.
Some cry, others look off across the quiet rolling landscape
and imagine the chaos of that great gettin'-up morning.
Many fan away the summer afternoon gnats
with the printed summary of my days
before shaking hands and hugging
and driving off to reassemble for ham, casseroles,
and sweet iced tea—a ritual feast
of recollection and anticipation.

Precaution

Watch where you tread
for what seems stable will
disappear.
You will drop like a whole cherry
falling between
ice cubes that collide
in a fresh glass of soda.

Street Market

Rib-thin strays linger,
wary someone
will drop scraps.

Vendors restack produce
or thumb multicolored bills
over misshapen paper sacks.

Flesh sellers swing, chop,
and cry out "Fresh!" to noisy air
smelling of decay and sunshine.

Dripping pregnant bags,
a bleached-knuckled shopper
stares at the busy stalls.

She mentally refolds
a forgotten list, sighs,
and turns toward home.

Clarification

"I'm flexible," I tell people.
I am not really flexible.
I like comfortable, day-to-day,
unbothered ordinariness.
Instead of "flexible,"
perhaps I should say,
"I am relatively unencumbered,"
which allows for repeated changes in life plans
whether I welcome them or not.

The Test

Hushed students bow reverently over prostrate sheets.
Some, inspired, furiously bruise the paper
with what they spent hours memorizing.
A few touch doubtful lips, eyes inscrutably lowered,
earnest prayers unanswered.
For long minutes all heads angle in unison,
then one, and then another, surfaces
to shake his cramped fingers,
or to rearrange a wisp of hair behind her ear,
or to glance anxiously up
where the secondhand glides in calm circles
above the creaking chairs and sighs of resignation
or of relief when the last question is filled out
and the bell releases everyone into the noisy bustle of the hall.

Requiem

He snacked on desiccated worms
discovered on the patio,
chirping crickets caught on the fly,
and the softer parts of field-fresh mice
(he left their stringy tails for me).

He also liked fish kibble.

He was just a tiny puff
of filthy fur under a bush
(all tiny claws, great hisses, and sad rheumy eyes)
when I first found him.

But for sixteen years thereafter
he reigned
the purring lord
of the sundrenched garden and my lap.

Recalcitrant

He's wailing like a lost soul behind the toilet,
emitting plaintive squeaks of lone desperation
that trail off into nothingness
as if he were condemned forever
to the company of the plumbing
and hadn't toys scattered about the room,
a full water bowl, ample food, a comfortable bed,
and a human more than willing to welcome him
should he decide to emerge from his cold ceramic confines.
I've tried luring him with pungent and delicious meats,
talking in a calming voice, and dangling a winsome
bit of string tipped with feathers and a small bell
in front of his cave, but he's having none of it,
and only emerges when I am safely out of
eye- and ear-shot. Sometimes late at night
I'll hear a crash as he rearranges items on the countertop
and I am reassured that he's mobile and mischievous.
The daily shovelfuls from the litter box
tell me that his bowels are in good order.
How long must I endure these wee cries of needless complaint
and celebrate his sandy-furred company only secondhand?

Cat Sick

Lights dance in her eyes.
Beneath the parietal dome,
her brain spins like a disco ball
or a Moroccan lantern whose
pierced metal emits colorful shards
onto a quiet whitewashed room.
She crouches to cough violently.
Though somewhat diluted by meat biscuits,
poison eats at her fangs
as she heaves fiber
onto a geometric rug.

Moon

The cat laps cream from the evening milking
and stretches into a pleased crescent on the straw,
curling her toes and talons in delight.
Her chin arcs to the farmer's calloused hand.
Stiff bovine limbs muster awkward hops
so as not to tread on this small purring predator.
The watchdog barks indignantly outside.
At home, the farmer's son practices the violin,
playing simple nursery songs;
his mother hums emphatically from the kitchen,
willing him to improve.
The stars quietly appear,
and the cat climbs to the hayloft,
curling into a perfect circle of grey
that vanishes into darkness.

Naptime Ritual

Stiff woven fibers pop
beneath determined claws.
A small pink bristled tongue
combs sandy brindled fur.
With a great jagged yawn,
the plump housecat curls
and hums herself to sleep.

Fusion

The pitted date squeezed
between mismatched pecan halves
dares the nut meats to blunt
its desert sweetness.

The Duel

A brace of tomcats began to curse at dawn
beneath my open bedroom window.
For half an hour, each summoned fiends from
the nine feline hells to sweep his rival away.
Staggering in my nightgown to the sash,
I groggily swore at both, but was ignored.
Suddenly, the larger beast rushed his enemy,
and pursued him up the empty street.
They then engaged with unsheathed claws,
and rolled out of sight, yowling, hissing,
intertwined in deadly combat.
The sun rose to bloody tufts of fur
littering the curb, the only evidence
(besides a throbbing headache)
of my sorely interrupted sleep.

Political Animal

She solicits my attention,
flirtatiously blinks her green eyes
and lounges in sunny spots
to be seen and admired.
When I am inattentive
she gives unequivocal hints—
cozies up and murmurs soothingly,
or rolls over, just out of reach,
to tempt me with a soft expanse of furry belly,
or nudges her polished bowl and caterwauls.
Refusing privacy, she waits for me to emerge
from my bath, to proffer reassuring treats
from the counter cork-topped jar.
Were I as good at lobbying,
I'd be powerful and rich—
or just another kept creature
like my cat.

Memes Old & New

Velvet legends
silently rock
bouffant hairdos

Poker-faced mutts
inspect their cards
at baize tables

Fat white-furred cats
float satisfied
loafed on glass

Tender fathers
shade young children
from heavy rain

Insomnia

An old doll with painted eyes
Balances the pump organ shelf

Over cigarette-stained creamy ivory
Her head bobbles on a spindle

Mother pulls down bad blood
To pierce a bursting fingertip

Rotten chunks of criminals
Attract clouds of flies

Paper houses collapse in flames
To waft shattered wishes skyward

Ashen leaves blow
Around a restless bed

Dad Jokes

Hatching rotten puns,
pre-counted unbearable,
fledged out not as foul.

Personal Library

Lint lingers on ridged leaves.
Stories crouch, ready to bundle you
into thread-bound worlds untroubled
by today's commercial margins
and frantic headlines.
Does modernity become clear
through antique texts?
Or are those ragged pages too opaque
for general enlightenment?

Barista

There's a pretty man behind the bar.
"May I help you?" he inquires,
ready to make a drink to our design.
We flock in to order, to admire
the careless scruff on his chin
and the high black bun from which his thick hair escapes.
He resembles some classical character in an old romance
when heroes were roughly muscled,
gently mannered,
and yet somehow had perfect teeth and no stink of sweat
after battling bandits and dragons.
In the aroma of freshly roasted beans we dream
that he could be as dashing as he looks.

Bangtan Corps

"Worldwide Handsome" looks
prompt excited fangirl squeals.
Honey-voiced onscreen,
seven men make whole armies
fall down in idol worship.

Sweet

Sterling parfait spoons
smear crystal bowls
with good dessert.
I am whipped cream
layered with fruit,
a failure at crunches.

Southern Barbeque

On a weather-beaten sign outside
an unassuming roadside shack,
the cartoon swine's cannibalistic delight
is directly proportional to the succulence
and serving size of pork pulled inside.
Sit at a derelict picnic table and
squirt sauce generously
from an unlabeled plastic bottle.
Drink a pint of syrup-sweet iced tea.
Scrape every morsel of hash from squeaking
Styrofoam with your undersized fork.
Sigh in pained contentment.
You have tasted the South.

Possession

Sometime in the 19th century,
with the end of "thee" in intimate formal use,
they gradually withered away to ghosts.
Sure, there were a few late-possessed in the 20th,
who displayed their freakishly archaic skill to the masses,
but as fragments of collective nostalgia.
Like the gods of old, devotees dwindling,
the power of poets dissolved, and they vanished from the West.
Poetry in English was not a serious component
of contemporary life.
In early adulthood, I was surprised to meet
several people who, bizarrely, claimed to write verse.
Didn't they know that this was as strange
as claiming to be a necromancer?
Nobody believed in their magic anymore.
A few persisted and even penned chants into a new millennium
about flowers, planets, and thwarted love.
So, maybe they were poets,
or knights without their shining armor,
or even dragons—
they all seemed equally mythical.
Then abruptly, in middle-age, I find myself also touched
with this literary whimsy.
An eagle did land on my head when I was six.
Once, while baby-sitting, I was attacked by a duck.
And at university I was spat upon by a songbird.
It seems these were omens
of eventual madness.

Making Do

"There's no money in poetry," I am repeatedly told.
This is God's honest truth.
Even the most laurelled versifiers
barely scrape by on visiting academic salaries,
or must needs ply secular trades in long, dull, daylight hours.
At night they drum and mutter
incantations to themselves over cluttered, lamplit desks,
while nearby spouses snore under blankets, books, and cats,
periodically waking to mumble,
"Honey, what are you doing? It's late."

About the Author

Born in Texas and raised in the Central Savannah River Area (CSRA) of Georgia, USA, Christina E. Petrides has taught English on Jeju Island, South Korea, since 2017.

Christina began writing poetry in 2018, and scores of her poems have since appeared in periodicals worldwide. *On Unfirm Terrain* is her first poetry collection.

Christina's first children's book, *Blueberry Man,* was issued in English in 2020 and in Korean in 2021, both by Tchaikovsky Family Books (Jeju). Christina's second children's book, *The Refrigerator Ghost,* was published in 2022 in Korean by Kong Publishers (Seoul).

Christina's website is: www.christinaepetrides.com

www.ingramcontent.com/pod-product-compliance
Lightning Source LLC
Chambersburg PA
CBHW070941160426
43193CB00011B/1770